BÔ YIN RÂ
(JOSEPH ANTON SCHNEIDERFRANKEN)

VOLUME 30
OF THE 32-VOLUME CYCLE

THE GATED GARDEN

LIFE IN THE LIGHT

For more information
about the books of Bô Yin Râ and
titles available in English translation
visit The Kober Press web site at
www.kober.com

THE KOBER PRESS PUBLISHES THE ONLY ENGLISH TRANSLATIONS
OF THE BOOKS OF BÔ YIN RÂ AUTHORIZED BY THE KOBER VERLAG,
SWITZERLAND. THE KOBER VERLAG PUBLISHES THE BOOKS OF
BÔ YIN RÂ IN THE ORIGINAL GERMAN AND HAS PROTECTED
THEIR INTEGRITY SINCE THE AUTHOR'S LIFETIME.

BÔ YIN RÂ
(JOSEPH ANTON SCHNEIDERFRANKEN)

LIFE IN THE
LIGHT

TRANSLATED FROM THE GERMAN
BY ERIC STRAUSS
EDITED BY MALKA WEITMAN

THE
KOBER
PRESS

BERKELEY, CALIFORNIA

CONTENTS

ACKNOWLEDGEMENTS

Special thanks to Jan Schymura, whose deep understanding of both the subtleties of the German language and the teachings of Bô Yin Râ has guided our work on this book. Jan reviewed our translations and made sure that we stayed true to the nuances of meaning in the German original.

Thanks also to David Peattie of BookMatters for his advice on book production.

And finally, much appreciation to the baristas at Berkeley's Cafe Roma for the many cups of cappuccino that enlivened our minds and spirits as we worked on these translations.

SELF-DISCLOSURE

For me to acknowledge who I am to myself
to say to those living with me on this earth
that I am different than they
To say that I am
what indeed I am
and have been through eternities
To bear witness from out of my eternal being
that humans too are anchored in Eternity—
all that I could only do when pressed
so that I finally was able to overcome
the resistance of my mortal self.

Hard years of struggle had to pass
but I emerged at last as master.
I had no choice but to prevail
if I would complete my work on earth
before time could destroy
this body made of flesh and blood.

♋

FUNDAMENTAL

I do not merely claim
to be what I am
I am it!
Independent of my opinion of myself
or the opinions of others.

But that which I am
I could not be
had I not forfeited the need
of my earthly being
to be admired
and given it over to the eternal Spirit.

No one can be that which I am
who still wants to be important
in his own eyes and the eyes of others
who share with him this time on earth.
All such vain delusion must fall away
if the primordial Being of Eternity
is to experience its self
within the time-bound mortal.

❧

QUESTION AND ANSWER

Are you the one who has returned?
No! I am one who has come for the first time.
No bringer of Light returns
even if while on earth
he might imagine he has returned.

What returns to evolving worlds
is the primordial Word
that, bathed in primordial Light
shines out from primordial Being.
The primordial Word
in which all "words" have their being
creates "sons" unto itself
eternally from out of the Eternal
and as Father is eternally with them in union
creating life eternal for those it has created.

In this way alone within the earthly realm
through those who offered eons past
to undertake this task
does the primordial Word reveal itself
to mortals—
enlightening those now on the earth
and all who later follow.

☙

UNION

I do not know how to tell you
when it was—
And even if I knew
earthly understanding could not comprehend
this measure of time.

I only know to say to you
that in the wide reaches of space
no star exists today
that was in being in that age
The age in which my earthly soul joined
with myself
the eternally living Luminary
with whom this soul today finds itself
in union
So that one life, sensing and experiencing
binds me—
the human mortal, my earthly soul,
and myself,
the being begotten of Eternity—
in indissoluble union
within the Spirit's realm.
Only the part of me
that came from the earth's soil
remains under the earth's spell
subject to decay and disintegration.

⁊

THREE IN ONE

I am always one within myself
yet also two
and in union we two are three
since each in union still remains:
himself
and the one with whom he has united
and at the same time also him
who has united both of them within himself.

In the earthly realm
where there is one
there cannot be a second
but in every Luminary
the one encloses in himself
not only just the other
but also both
within his unity.

☙

WHO I AM AND WHO I AM NOT

I am not a seer
who believes in what he "sees."
I am not an ecstatic
whose ecstasy
robs him of judgment.
I am not a poet who
accountable to no one
creates an über world
to suit his art and whim.
I am not a thinker
who thinks up a world
as it reveals itself
to the rational mind.

I am forever immersed
in *eternal* life
and my words relate
the Truth that only eternal Reality holds
the Truth that remains Truth
even as the mortal body grows cold
and no thought moves the brain
that once held this Truth dear.

৵

IDENTICAL

When I speak to you
there speaks
the one begotten of the Spirit
and his messenger
the one bowed with the earth's burdens
in whom the soul can here be found
that once eons ago
joined me in the Spirit's realm.

Yet the eternal one
and the earthly messenger
can no longer be separated
here where they with loving
mutual recognition
bring together and unite
within the soul
the primordial earthly energies
with the divine—
one whole for all Eternity.

Thus I am since all eternities
the one begotten of the Spirit
and I also am today
within this realm of time
the one bowed with the earth's burdens.

※

DESTINY

I am not the "way" for you the way a stream
that surges from the mountains
becomes a path for every ship
that would reach the ocean.

I became a path for you
out of *earth* and out of *stone*
but recognizable only to those
who, in their own selves, in their own time,
are destined to find me as the path.

Thus, I myself
am left without a choice—
I only can direct the steps of those
who, within themselves,
recognize me as their path
and with hearts prepared to receive the Light
absorb my words.

❧

IF I AM TO BE YOUR PATH

If I am to be your path
then I must stir your soul
and bring up from its primal depths
the soul experiences within your innermost
so that they enter into your awareness
and are lifted onto the Eternal Realm.

If I am to be your path
you must learn to find your selves
through me
and yet must not distance your selves
from yourselves.

If I am to be your path
you *yourselves* must walk
the way I must teach you to walk
if I would see you enter into the Light.

If I am to be your path
I must ask you from my heart
never to forget
how foolish it would be
and how presumptuous to expect
to experience here on earth
what is only given to the Luminary
who lives in the Light
in order that all whom his word reaches
may be lifted up
and reunited with God in the Eternal Realm.

❦

CALLED TO SHOW THE WAY

Not to keep you believing in the delusion
that intellect can create Being
not to raise up holy writ and dogma
not to satisfy idle curiosity
have I been called to show you the way
into the Spirit's Light
into the timeless nature that is God's
which you can only comprehend
if in deepest silence and with reverence
your soul approaches it.

My words are meant to teach your feelings
to sense what is *true*
and as a true reflection
of divine unfolding
to challenge
false conceptions about God.
What I, in the Eternal Realm
have experienced of God
is meant to keep you from idolatry and sin.

◌◦

GOD

In all forms
both the one who forms and the form itself.
In all life
both creation and that which preserves it.
In unity holding
all numbers in their fullness
God is content
and the content's container.

The Eternal One
sets time
within space
for himself
and yet
remains timeless.

☙

ETERNAL UNION

Primordial Being
is female being
and male being.

Everything that emanates from out of
Primordial Being
is female being and male being
in an infinite variety of blendings.

Those who believe
that God is male being alone
are far distant from truth!
God is female being as well as male being.
The Father is primordial feminine
as well as primordial masculine
eternally renewing themselves—
the eternal union of both poles of creation.

༄

ONE WITHIN THE OTHER

The Father
lives within Primordial Being
and as Primordial Light
pours itself
into Primordial Word
from out of which the Father
self-created
lives his Self
and raises up
all those who are luminous in him
to Primordial Light.

In the same way
all live one within the other
who in the Father
live out of the Father
and all are given in the Father
Being and Light and Word.

๛

INFINITELY VARIED UNITY

Eternally One
in himself
is the Father.
Yet he embraces two ways of being
since he is both female and male.

And at the same time
as Being and Light and Word
unfolding in three aspects
he remains himself his own.

In this same way also
he is the great Four:
four aspects, each equal to the other
directing spiritual impulses
spiritual events.

And he is
tenfold in himself
the primal spiritual Powers
that emanate from his being
that form all forms.

And twelvefold the Fathers
the sources of all revelation
who each within the unity of the twelve
himself remains the one Father
the eternal, united One
each his own testament to this truth
and in spiritual form
embodied.

From out of this testament
all Luminaries proceed
who in the fullness of time
follow their guide
to find humans on earth
who are destined for Light.

In this way, the many
find their way back to the eternal One
who is eternally in the process of renewal
burning in the brightest fires of love
encompassing all numbers
manifesting in an infinite variety of forms
and united in Oneness.

❧

OMNIPOTENCE

Law unto himself
beholden only to himself
as Primordial Being
deepest black night
that lightens to Primordial Light—
as Primordial Being
strictest silence
that speaks itself as Primordial Word—
thus the Eternal One
encompasses all power
and cherishes within
that which has issued from that power.

But wherever the innermost of all that *is*
has hardened and become
the outermost
there God, in his omnipotence,
denies himself many powers.
And in the material realm
where physical forms manifest
where earthly events occur
these powers must now
reside in that material realm.

In all creation and destruction
the power embedded in the universe
and made a gift to all
now guides the drives and strivings

of all physical bodies
and it alone determines what shall live
and what shall die.

❧

MASTERING THE SENSES

Those who presume
to call themselves wise
have told you
that this ever-changing earth
is a delusion
a mirage of the senses
believed in by the misguided.

They say that those who cannot
free themselves
from the allure of the senses
will never free themselves
from the illusions
which they themselves created
that bind them
to their beliefs about the earth.

Those who teach these things
are truly slaves of their senses.
Because whoever fears
the power of the senses
has surely not become their master
nor awakened in the world of Spirit
that lies beyond the senses.

☙

EXTRA-SENSORY

Aspects of Reality
that earthly senses cannot perceive
are called "extra-sensory"
for good reason.
Yet one should not believe
that what cannot be grasped by earthly senses
could, in the world of Spirit, be perceived
without their spiritual equivalent.

When referring to these spiritual senses
one may speak of "super-senses"
for good reason.
For these spiritual senses
perform the same functions
in the realm of the Eternal Spirit
as our body's earthly senses do
here on earth.

☙

SPIRITUAL AWARENESS

The reach of your perceptions and beliefs
determines what you will experience.
The borders of your earthly experience
are set by your own self.
The earthly senses can only convey to you
the knowledge
that corresponds to the perceptions
and beliefs
you hold already
and what is not encompassed by them
will not be present for you.
Nor can the keenest senses
let you comprehend
what lies beyond those limits.
Such limits none may cross.

It is the same in the realm of Spirit.
Here too the keenest spiritual senses
can never cross the borders
the soul sets for itself.
The soul will only experience
what fits within the limits of those borders:
All else will not be present for it.

In the realm of Spirit progress means:
a transformation of the soul's perceptions
and beliefs.
And those who would transform them
know what they must do

to subdue the dark powers
that struggle to possess the soul.

Those who ask for help
in the silence of their inner being
will receive it within
and will perceive in their souls
awareness expanded
until their spiritual senses
are no longer limited
and now allow them to experience within
timeless Reality.

⁜

ONLY THEN

Even though you earnestly desire it
you no longer know
how to find God
because your senses are bound
by concepts that came from others
and by those that come from your own self.

All too many humans
have forgotten how to search for God
within themselves
and all the while there are those
who long ago have given up the search
in despair.

You must overcome within yourselves
the concepts that now bind you.
Only then may you hope to find God
within yourselves.

෴

FEAR

Many who search for God
would have found what they were seeking
long ago
had not their souls been bound by fear.

They have heard God proclaimed to be
avenger of all sins
and know themselves to be
stained by sin and burdened by its weight.

They believe that they are doomed
and born for damnation.
They fear themselves condemned
by the One who sees and judges everything.

They stretch out their arms
in supplication
and beg for mercy
but do not dare to lift themselves
to life in God.

This curse of fear must first be overcome
before at last they may find
the One
who is Love itself
and never will forget whoever also loves.

❧

GIVING AND RECEIVING

Not until you lose yourself in God
will you find God within.

Until you have awakened in God
the senses of your soul
remain bound to the Dream.

Only when you have given over
your own self
can God
permeate your being.

Once you have surrendered
and lost yourself in God
then, on a holiest of nights,
your Living God will be born in you.

❧

INDESCRIBABLE

Just as on earth
we experience space
only within time
so too in the Eternal Realm
those filled with Love
perceive things in a certain way.

Each word that issues from the mouth of God
is space
and all of time
is bound up within space
and is perceived by every soul
as space enfolded.

And yet—
experience in the Eternal Realm
cannot be described in words
of any earthly tongue.
And those who try to do so
can only use imagery and symbols
to hint at what those alone experience
who have awakened within God.

❧

ENLIGHTENMENT

Our understanding of earthly matters grows
from perceiving through the body's senses
through reasoning
based on concepts and associations.
But comprehension in the realm
of the Eternal—
comprehension of a primal sort—
comes about, eternally
as a filling of the space within the soul
that has prepared itself to receive Light.

Revelation of this sort
comes only to the soul that has left
its earthly body.
On earth it comes to those
begotten of the Spirit only—
those who, like myself, though living
on this earth
can see, as is natural to their kind
within the space of their own soul
within the light of Love that is their own
the Infinite, the Eternal.

To all of you, however, for whom I write
this legacy
and for those who will follow you
a different spiritual experiencing is allotted
as long as you sojourn here on this earth.

❦

LIFE IN THE LIGHT

Life in the Light
can only come into being
in regions
begotten and formed by Light.
Here time
is enfolded within space.
All of time
has been poured into space
and all of space
is life unbroken
lived in Light
lovingly devoted to Light.

Experience and knowing
become one within Being
and enter the soul
as space
the soul that itself is space
that in itself
embraces time
and in which Light
reveals itself
as space.

❧

TRANSFORMATION

In the light that wells
from out of the primordial Light
and like primordial Light
is space when formed
all impulses arising in the soul
transform themselves
into forms within space
filled with energy and animated by Light
that interpenetrate
and act on each other
each recognizing and experiencing the other
and yet retaining the form
that speaks what they are.

Here thoughts formed in the brain
can no longer be found—
thoughts the earthly human being needs
for understanding
and to form ideas.
Here the soul transforms itself
into that which it now understands
that which it sought to understand
while still on earth
by giving it a name.

❧

THE SOUL

The soul can be an ocean
pure and alive and in motion
but also a puddle
polluted and filled with earthly clutter.

When it is an ocean
it is in unending movement,
cleansing and renewing itself.
When it is a lake, it is also alive
and in motion
purifying itself.
And even when a pond, it can clear its waters
although it may take long for clutter
to settle
after storms have stirred it up.

But when the soul is a puddle
refuse of every sort collects
and it becomes a quagmire of decay
no longer even aware of what it has become.

❧

MORE ABOUT THE SOUL

The soul can be a cathedral
but also a pigsty
a narrow stall
or a universe...

Through everything it gives away
and everything that it takes in
its inner form, its essence,
and ability to evolve is determined.

The soul can only absorb
that which is in harmony with it.
That which is not in harmony
must be calmly left aside.

Everything that expands
the spaciousness of the soul
is a blessing
and the soul in turn
will send out blessings.

But the soul must always guard
against envy, hate, and loveless hardness
because these shrink its space
and can narrow it to nothingness.

৵

THE DEPARTED

They have left
as they had come.
They had given
they had taken
and yet
could not preserve
a single token from the earth.

When the mortal body grows cold,
it detaches from its mortal soul—
the earthly soul that once shaped
the nature of the being
who lived inside this body—
the soul that sustained that being
and enlivened its experiences
while on this earth.

Only what the *timeless* soul
begotten of the Spirit
had gained on earth
does not dissolve
in death's embrace.
What the departed
take with them
from their time on earth
is the shape they gave
to their immortal soul.

❧

NEAR AND FAR

Those who left the earth
but are still bound to it
by bonds forged by time—
those who have not yet
liberated their souls—
have nonetheless
not all reached the same inner state
nor can they all hear the same call.

Some remain lost
reliving their former lives on earth
while others have left earthly experience
and earthly goals
far behind
and so are closer to the Light.

Thus, some are near
to the radiant Light
while others still abide
within earth's darkling
density.

໑

INEFFABLY CLOSE

Those who, through the transformation
that is the fate of all begotten of the earth
are now no longer visible
no longer felt or seen by earthly senses
are, nonetheless, from within the realm
of souls
closer to us who truly love them
than they were
during their time on earth.

Even if at first
in their existence in the other realm
they remain bound up with earthly illusions
and day-dreams
and have not yet found deliverance
from all that is no longer relevant
to where they now are—
they soon will learn
as they reside in the soul-space
and experience their souls as space
to recognize that sacred space within
the souls that still remain
embodied on the earth.
And through that space
they draw ineffably close
to those still tied to the realm of time.

❦

LIFE IN ETERNITY

Life in the realm of Eternity
is not like living in a kind of time
that is different than time on earth
and yet is time nonetheless.
Here every moment of life—
if one may borrow a term
from life in earthly time—
is filled with the Eternal
with Reality begotten of the Spirit.

Many have walked the path
that leads through the gateway of time
to pass from the life lived as time
and into the life lived as space.
And yet...
not all were ready to lift themselves
upward
by taking the hand of a Helper
to receive life as lived in Eternity
and to now at last begin to live.

Only when they have laid aside
all the goals they had on earth
will they, hand in hand with their Helper,
find life in Eternity.

❧

FULFILLMENT

Only when the soul that has departed
from this earth
finds nothing more within itself
whether bad or good
that binds it still to life on earth
Only then can it lift itself up to the Light
And from that eternal realm
view its former life
illuminated, free of earthly strivings
reflected back to it
clearly, the way it truly was.

Here the mystery-filled turning point
takes place
when every soul receives the revelation
and comes to know the mission that the Spirit
has ordained for it.
In soul-space bathed in Light eternal
the soul, now shining forth with Spirit's Love
experiences its fulfillment
everlasting.

∽

For a deeper understanding
of the core of Bô Yin Râ's teachings
you may want to read:

The Book on the Living God,
The Book on Life Beyond and
The Book on Human Nature

These three books should be
read together.

A description of all three books follows.

The Book on the Living God

The Book on the Living God describes the inner path that leads to birth of the Living God within—what we must do and what to avoid on the long journey towards awakening the consciousness of our timeless self.

Ordinary consciousness, Bô Yin Râ tells us, is actually like sleep; there is a greater consciousness that is alive in us, informing every cell, and our task is to unite it with our self-awareness.

We must also set aside the ideas we have been taught about an anthropomorphic God. God is not meant to be an external object of worship but, rather, an experience to be awakened within us. We are cautioned to avoid the pitfalls that might divert us: following false teachers or believing that certain foods or exercises, or ecstatic experiences, have spiritual merit. Everyday life, when lived with attention to the ultimate goal, will lead us towards a gradual awakening of our timeless self.

Contents: *Word of Guidance. "The Tabernacle of God is with Men." The White Lodge. Meta-Physical Experiences. The Inner Journey. The En-Sof. On Seeking God. On Leading an Active Life. On "Holy Men" and "Sinners." The Hidden Side of Nature. The Secret Temple. Karma. War and Peace. The Unity among Religions. The Will to Find Eternal Light. The Human Being's Higher Faculties of Knowing. On Death. On the Spirit's Radiant Substance. The Path toward Perfection. On Everlasting Life. The Spirit's Light Dwells in the East. Faith, Talismans, and Images of God. The Inner Force in Words. A Call from Himavat. Giving Thanks. Epilogue.*

The Book on Life Beyond

The Book on Life Beyond is a guide to help readers understand what they can expect to find in the life beyond death, and how to best prepare for it.

Bô Yin Râ explains that life beyond is actually another dimension of the same life we know here on earth—just as real and solid, but perceived through spiritual, rather than our limited, physical senses. He emphasizes the direct connection between our actions here on earth and their effects on life beyond. We bring with us into life beyond the same state of inner being with which we departed, and are able to experience its wonders exactly to the degree to which we have developed our spiritual self. For example, those who have failed to show compassion for others and have lived selfishly will find that life beyond lacks the warmth and light that other, more developed souls can perceive.

Bô Yin Râ counsels us to mentally practice the "art of dying" as a meditative practice to prepare for the transition from physical to spiritual existence. The goal is to constantly orient one's thinking, emotions and desires toward transformation of the self, in order to be able to receive the spiritual help that will be available to us after death.

Contents: *Introduction. The Art of Dying. The Temple of Eternity and the World of Spirit. The Only Absolute Reality. What Should One Do?*

The Book on Human Nature

The Book on Human Nature presents basic concepts about human nature with the goal of inspiring readers to awaken the timeless, spiritual spark within. We become fully human only when the spiritual potential within us gradually awakens and infuses our material, purely animal selves. It is a path that every human being may and should pursue.

A central understanding is that all life results from the joining of opposites, in particular, the polarity of male and female energies. Bô Yin Râ emphasizes that the true spiritual human being is male and female united in one entity; when we seek our spiritual self, we must call forth the male and female in ourselves and in all things. He discusses the biblical fall from grace as a descent from the spiritual plane, in which male and female were united, onto a material plane, in which male and female are split apart.

Bô Yin Râ warns men that holding onto the illusion of male superiority means forfeiting their spiritual life. While the spiritual paths that are natural for men and women are different in tone—open and receptive for women, active and grasping for men—they are equal and complementary. He tells us that *true* marriage is preparation for the life beyond: by coordinating the desires, wills and attitudes of two beings we once again bring about, in some measure, the original state in which male and female energies are united.

Contents: *Introduction. The Mystery Enshrouding Male and Female. The Path of the Female. The Path of the Male. Marriage. Children. The Human Being of the Age to Come. Epilogue. A Final Word.*

THE
KOBER
PRESS